"Our definition of a work of art as something beautiful, skill-fully made to give pleasure, applies as truly to the artistic industries as it does to the Fine Arts. It is not enough that the thing should seem beautiful to the maker, there must be a corresponding perceptive faculty in the person or class for whom it is made"

"Between the artists' land and the world of every-day life hangs many a spangled rainbow bridge. He that can traverse the intervening gulf will assuredly find his way to the realm where all the poets and painters and musicians have dwelt, and where they have beheld the glimpses of beauty, which, though perhaps but dimly remembered and indistinctly embodied in their works, have become the priceless possessions of the human race"

—W. M. CONWAY, "*Domain of Art,*" pp. 79-88.

WHATEVER of artistic satisfaction lies in Rookwood is due first to the individuality of its artists, to their freedom of expression in the ever-changing language of an art that never repeats itself, that has in each vase some new message of beauty. Rookwood cannot be understood without an appreciation of its radical difference from commercial industries Its whole history and development centres upon the one idea of individualism, the entire absence of duplication, and the constant progress toward new forms of artistic expression.

The origin of Rookwood dates back thirty years to experiments in making pottery undertaken by a number of women of Cincinnati. One of them, Mrs. Maria Longworth Storer, finally built in 1880 a pottery of her own, which she called "Rookwood", the name of her father's country place near Cincinnati. The idea was to produce, with our native clay a new pottery original and different from all others, by applying color decoration in the material itself before firing, and then to protect and enrich this with appropriate glazes

In 1883 Mr. William Watts Taylor assumed active direction of the works, in 1890 Mrs. Storer transferred to him her interest and he formed a company to develop and perpetuate what she had started

As Rookwood was not imitating other wares, but starting as a pioneer along new lines, it had to work out its own processes and its own style Instead of importing foreign decorators with fixed methods Rookwood gathered to itself a staff of American artists and bravely set out to solve its own problems. These artists year after year progressed in mastering the new decorative medium, making their own technique and working out styles so individual that signatures upon the pieces are hardly needed to identify them.

From its foundation to the present time Rookwood has kept itself free from those commercial influences which are destructive to artistic qualities Its workers have depended upon their own initiative and originality of invention.

Thus Rookwood has grown into a highly organized community of workers, to which it supplies the most advanced resources of a very complicated craft. It does this as a means to the freest expression of individual artists who associate themselves with it and whose signatures appear upon its productions.

THE ART OF ROOKWOOD.

The conditions under which objects of art can be made are necessarily different from those governing manufactures Where artistic expression is the first consideration financial return must be secondary While the Rookwood Pottery Company is a business organization it is deliberately operated at a minimum profit, in order that its staff of artists may have the utmost latitude in the creation of new and ever-varying objects of art. Any one familiar with art knows what it means to put new thought, new life, new expression into each piece of work, day after day and year after year That Rookwood has done this without wavering for a quarter of a century is its greatest distinction

A vase made at Rookwood under the conditions existing there is as much an object of art as a painted canvas or sculpture in marble or bronze And the artist's signature upon the vase is as genuine a guarantee of originality An object of art is immeasurably more precious when its owner knows there is no other just like it, that the particular artistic conception expressed there will never again be found quite the same. A Rookwood artist never does two vases alike, but carefully studies, composes and works out each piece for itself. It is that creative process which makes a piece of Rookwood an object of art.

Adherence to these high aims has enabled Rookwood to attain its high rank among the world's ceramics and to win recognition from the best judges of pottery as being a distinct artistic creation, to which they have awarded the highest honors at the world's great expositions.

The gold medal gained at Paris, in 1889, was followed by the highest award at the World's Columbian Exposition, in Chicago, 1893, the gold medal at the Pan-American Exposition, at Buffalo; the Grand Prix at Paris in 1900, the world's highest honor; and two Grand Prizes at the Louisiana Purchase Exposition, St. Louis, 1904, the highest awards made.

"IRIS"

THE EIGHT TYPES OF ROOKWOOD.

The many-sided development of Rookwood has naturally given rise to a variety of types, each of which distinctly differs from the others. Experiments are constantly being made to produce new bodies and glazes to meet the ever-changing demands of the artists. The clays used are entirely American and largely from the Ohio Valley. In the earlier years the native clays first inclined the color quality toward yellows, browns and reds, all of which the transparent glazes sought to merge into a deep yellow tone. The larger command of material and the knowledge gained by past experiments soon evolved new types and a greater perfection of glaze and decoration until to-day the latest types of Rookwood differ greatly from its first production.

"STANDARD"

Is the name given to that widely known type of Rookwood which was first produced at the pottery. It is noted for its low tones, usually yellow, red and brown in color, with flower decoration, characterized by a luxuriant painting in warm colors under a brilliant glaze From a comparatively light and golden color scheme the arrangement varies to deep rich red, brown, and green combinations in mellow tones The ware of this type is richer and more brilliant than ever before.

"SEA GREEN"

Is characterized by a limpid, opalescent, sea green effect. A favorite decoration is of fish moving under water. In floral designs under this glaze, blues, yellows, and sometimes reds are used. Beautiful combinations of rich blues and greens, relieved with glowing touches of golden yellow, red, and other warm colors mark this type.

"IRIS"

Is a light type with deliciously tender and suggestive color effects under a brilliant white glaze. In the "Iris" the variety and range of colors is practically unlimited, rich and warm as well as cool and delicate ones being attained in pieces of equal beauty.

"STANDARD"

The methods of preparation are the same as in the "Standard" type, with such modifications as came naturally from the light body decorated in delicate greys, pinks, soft blues, greens, and yellows. The "Iris" has a real pottery quality, a softness quite other than that of porcelain, a mellowness in fact that marks it as "Rookwood", distinct from other makes of light ware.

"MAT GLAZES"

The "Mat Glazes" are distinguished by the absence of gloss. Their texture is in itself delightful, a pleasure to the eye and to the touch, whether the surface be decorated or not. The glaze is no longer designed merely to protect the colors beneath, nor to reveal them as though swimming in a lustrous depth, but is now itself the dominating interest.

Rookwood Mat possesses hitherto unknown range of color in glazes of astonishing variety of texture. Now it seems solid as quartz, and partaking of its crystalline structure; again one sees a more mellow surface, suggesting that of firm, ripe fruit; or again, it suggests the quality of old ivory, or of stained parchment; but always showing a slight translucency, a sense of depth, and a pleasure in the feel of it which makes it delightful to the touch.

On many pieces decoration is applied of flowers or other subjects, broadly painted or modeled. Others are treated with simple incised designs, yet always emphasizing those qualities of texture and color which give this type of Rookwood its fine distinction.

"MAT GLAZE PAINTING."

Is a mat glaze with decorations painted in rich, warm reds, yellows, greens, and blues, a process of the greatest difficulty, suggestive of flowing enamels, but with a mat texture.

"CONVENTIONAL MAT GLAZE."

This type is a mat glaze with flat, conventional decoration in colors. This new type of Rookwood appeals to a taste for simple, flat decorations rather than naturalistic treatment, and reflects an important movement in modern art.

"SEA GREEN"

"INCISED MAT GLAZE."

Derives its name from the incised decoration. This type is made in reds, blues, yellows, greens, etc., in a multitude of shapes; sometimes in single colors, sometimes in a combination of two or more colors.

For daily use in the effective arrangement of flowers throughout the seasons a collection of Rookwood Mat Vases offers endless opportunity for harmonious combinations.

"MODELED MAT GLAZE."

This type of Rookwood has colored mat glazes, combining richness of color with softness of texture and modeled decoration, in a great variety of beautiful designs. Vases of this kind are sometimes mounted as lamps or electroliers.

"VELLUM WARE."

This variety of Rookwood Mat Glaze differs from all others, and was first exhibited at the St. Louis Exposition, 1904. It is the fruit of long experiment, and technically considered, is an achievement worthy to be first shown at a World's Exposition, so radical is the departure it makes from any previously known types.

The name Vellum conveys some idea of its refinement of texture and color. Devoid of lustre, without dryness, it partakes both to the touch and to the eye of the qualities of old parchment. The Mat Glazes hitherto known have permitted, by reason of their heaviness, of but little decoration other than modeling or very flat and broad painting. The refinements of rendering so generally esteemed in ceramics have been impossible in that medium. The Vellum on the contrary retains for the artist all those qualities possible hitherto under brilliant glaze alone. It is therefore within bounds to say that Rookwood, in developing this new ware, has taken a step forward as remarkable as any in its history.

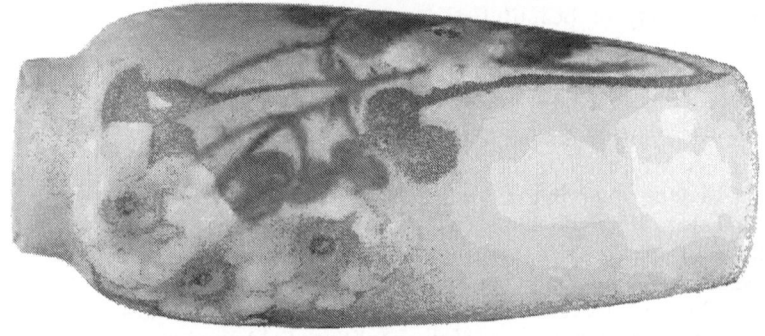

"IRIS"

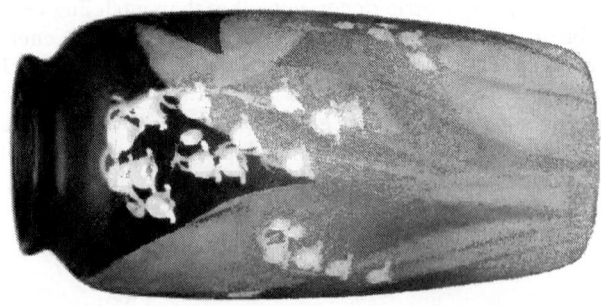

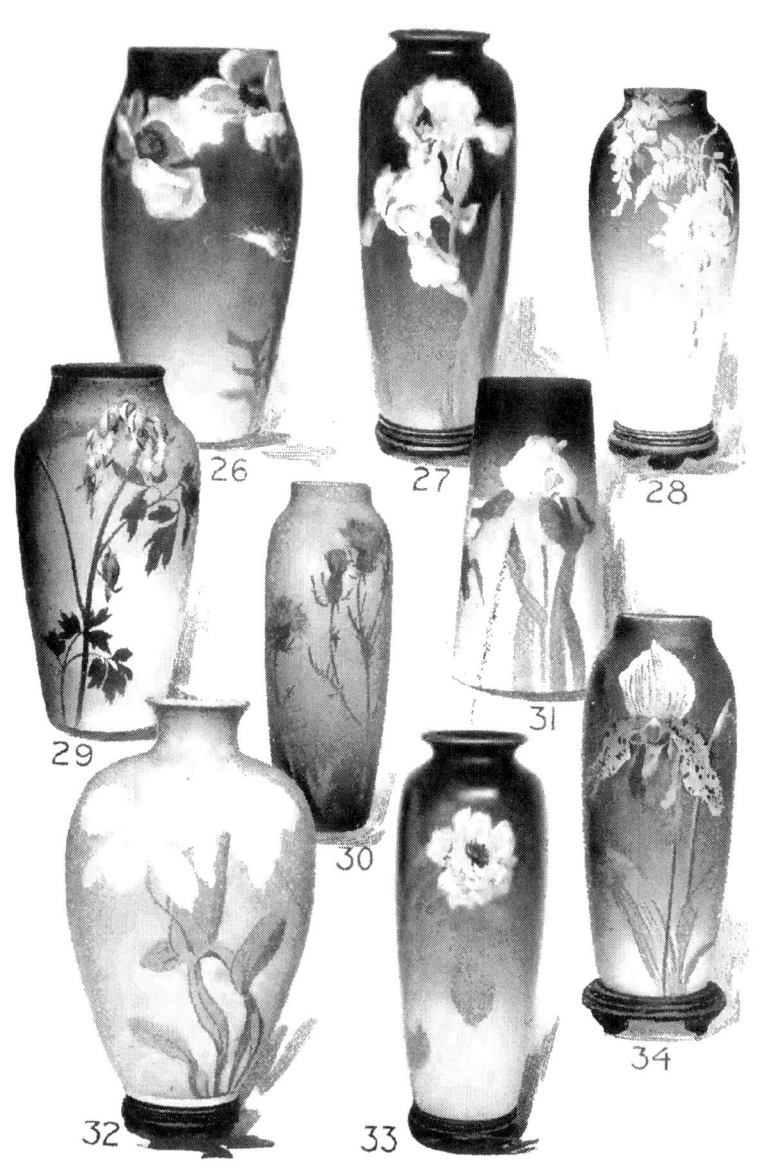

26
27
28
29
30
31
34
32
33

HOW TO ORDER ROOKWOOD.

As no piece of Rookwood is ever duplicated, it is impossible to issue a catalogue in the ordinary sense of the term

The pieces illustrated in this book were in the pottery studios at the time the Rookwood Book was issued, but possibly when you receive this copy there may not remain unsold a single one of these pieces. The Rookwood Book will nevertheless serve as a guide in ordering Rookwood.

If you desire any of the pieces of Rookwood illustrated, specify those you would like to see, and we will express pieces of the same type, as nearly as possible like the ones you have selected in form, size and price, either to some local dealer, or to you direct, with the privilege of examining the pieces sent, selecting such as you wish to purchase, and returning the others to the pottery. This is the only way in which we are able to supply Rookwood in places where we have no local representative, and it has been uniformly satisfactory

Rookwood is made in such a great variety of designs and decorations that the range for selection is practically unlimited. While we will never duplicate a piece, we can send you another, often by the same artist, equal in every way to the one illustrated. It is important that you should read the descriptions carefully in order to write us definitely what you wish; and we shall take every care to meet your wishes. In any case we extend to you in this way the opportunity of seeing the piece before you buy it The Rookwood Book is sent to you as the best available method of placing before lovers of beautiful pottery a clear idea of what Rookwood is in its different types, glazes, decorations and prices.

No real work of art is valued according to its size, but by its quality. Thus, a Rookwood vase which is small in size, may be so rare in design, decoration, glaze and quality, due to the eccentricities of the fire, that it will frequently have a greater artistic value than a piece many times larger. And again, two vases of the same size may vary widely in price, according to the artist who paints the design upon the piece, or the varying conditions which affect the cost of its production.

"MAT GLAZE PAINTING"

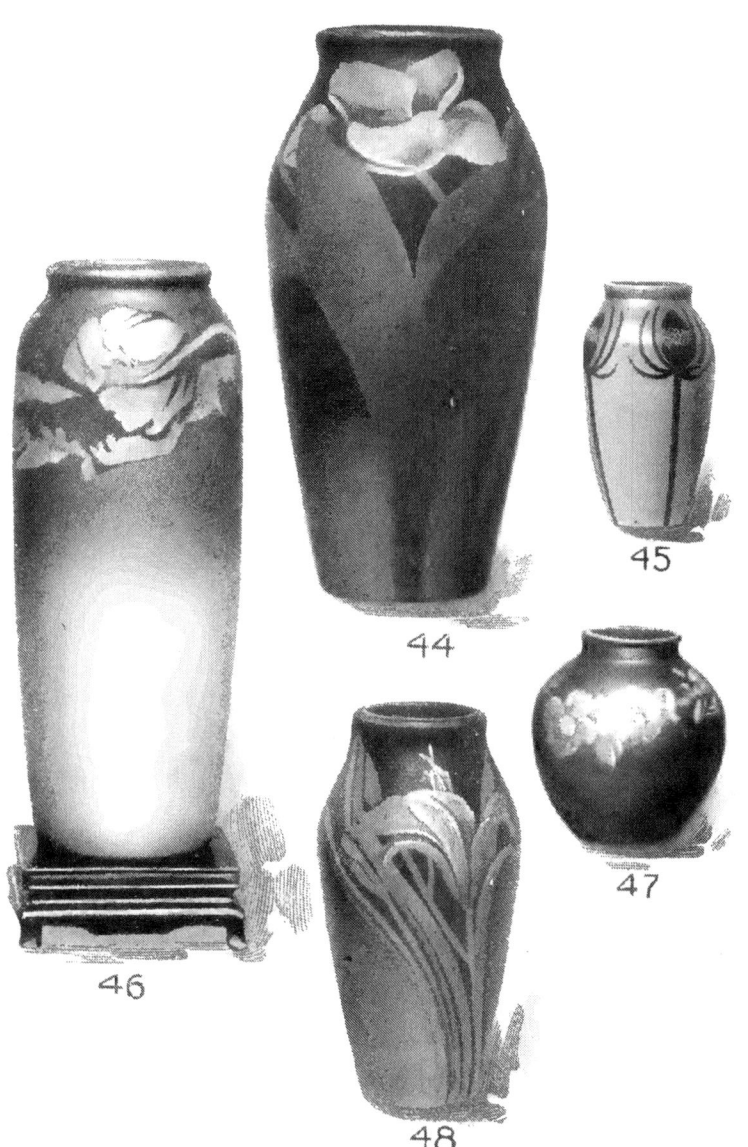

44

45

46

47

48

49

50

51

52

53

Rookwood Honors

The Twelfth Annual Exhibition, (London 1887), of Paintings on China   **Special Mention.**

Pottery and Porcelain Exhibition of the Pennsylvania Museum, Memorial Hall, Philadelphia, November, 1888, **First Prize** for "Pottery, Modeled and Decorated", and **First Prize** for "Painting Underglaze".

Exhibition of American Art Industry, Pennsylvania Museum Memorial Hall, Philadelphia, November, 1889, (Pottery and Porcelain Section)   **First Prize** Gold Medal for Faience.

Exposition Universelle, Paris, 1889, **Gold Medal.**

World's Columbian Exposition, Chicago, 1893, **Highest Award.** Also exhibited in the Fine Arts Building by invitation

Exposition Universelle, Paris, 1900, **Grand Prix.**

International Exhibition of Ceramics, St Petersburg, 1901, **Grand Prix.**

Pan-American Exposition, Buffalo, 1901, **Gold Medal.** Highest Award.

Charleston, S. C, Exposition, 1902, **Gold Medal**   Highest Award.

Turin, Italy, International Exposition of Modern Decorative Art, 1902, **Diploma of Honor.** Highest Award.

Louisiana Purchase Exposition, St. Louis, 1904, **Two Grand Prizes.**

"CONVENTIONAL
AND INCISED
MAT GLAZES"

54

55

56

57

58

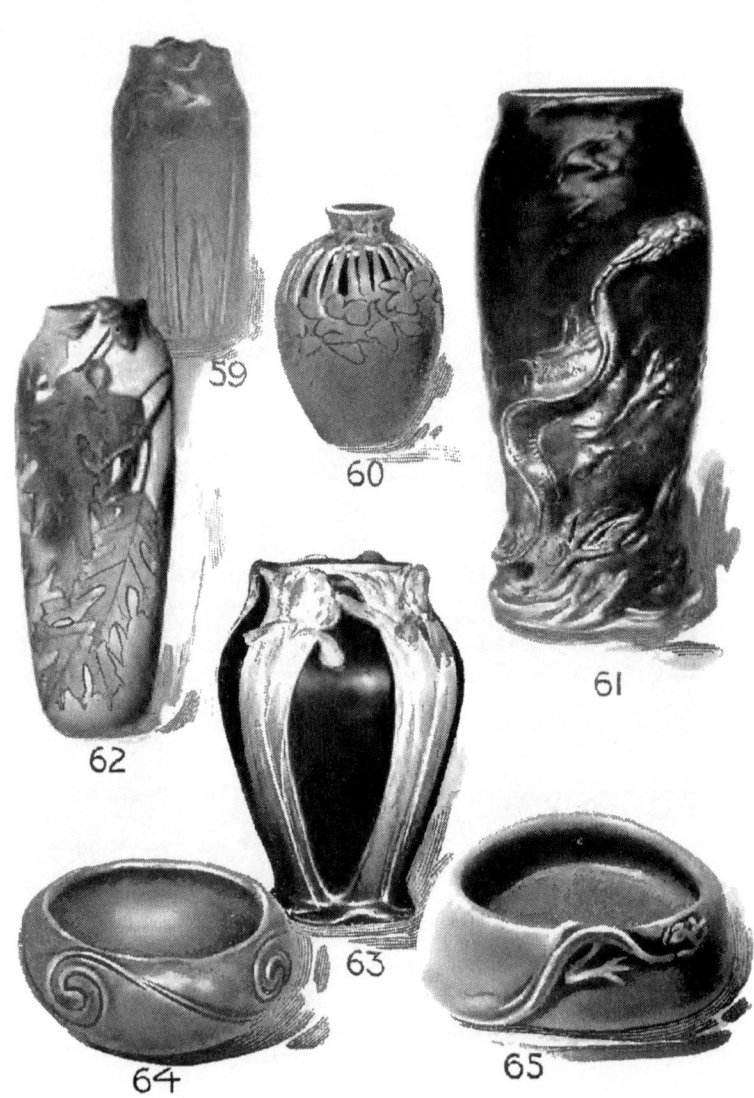

59

60

61

62

63

64

65

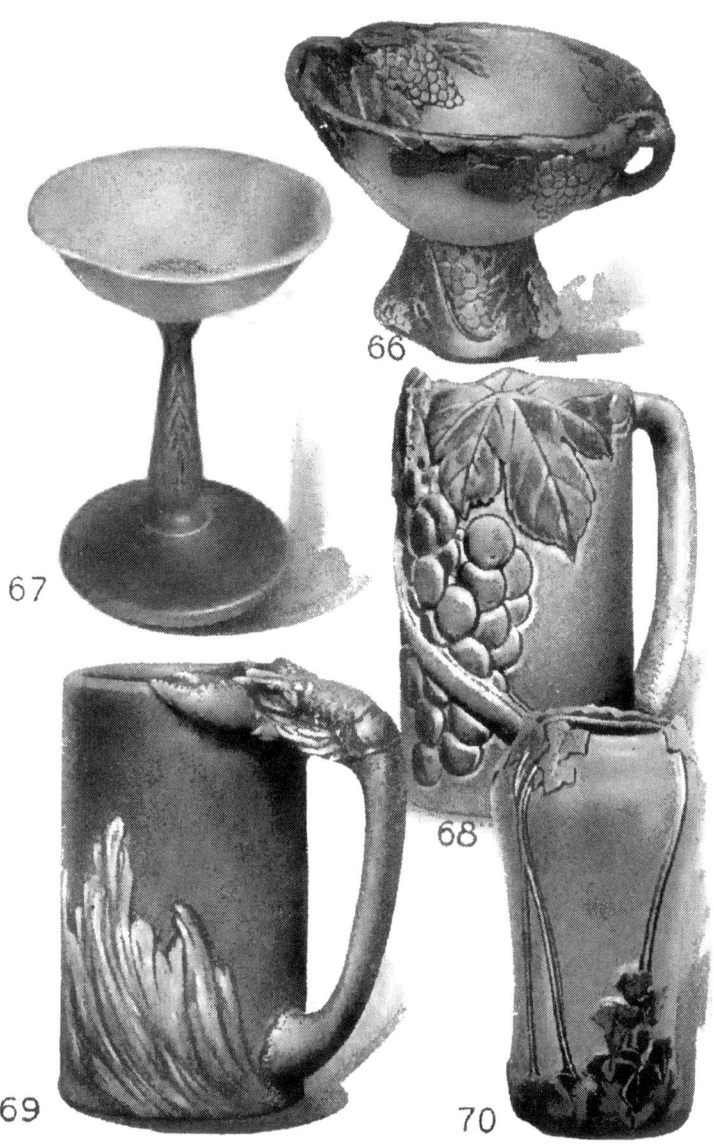

66

67

68

69

70

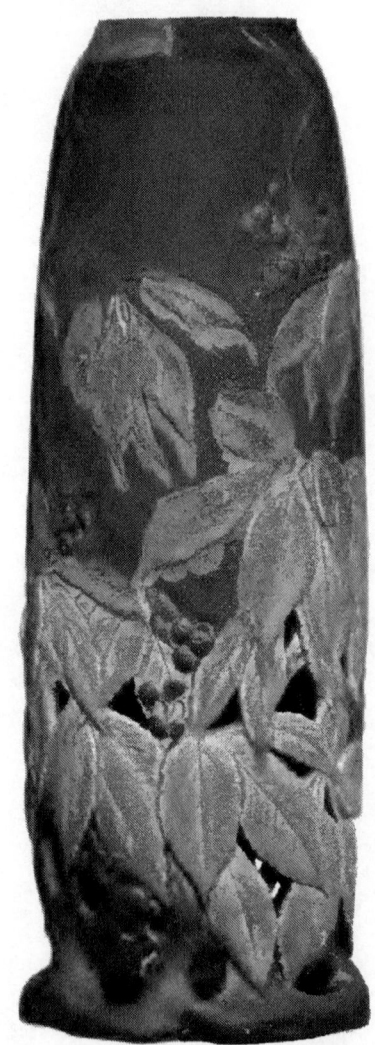

"MODELED MAT GLAZE"

71

72

73

74

75

76

77

78

79

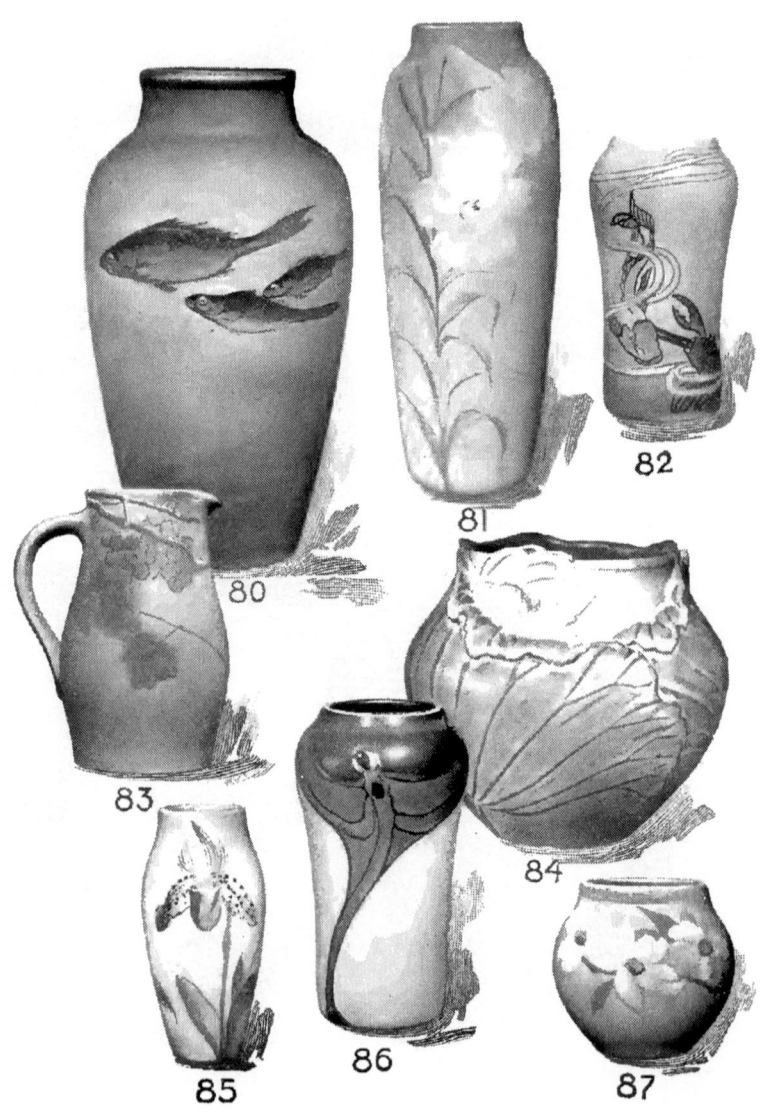

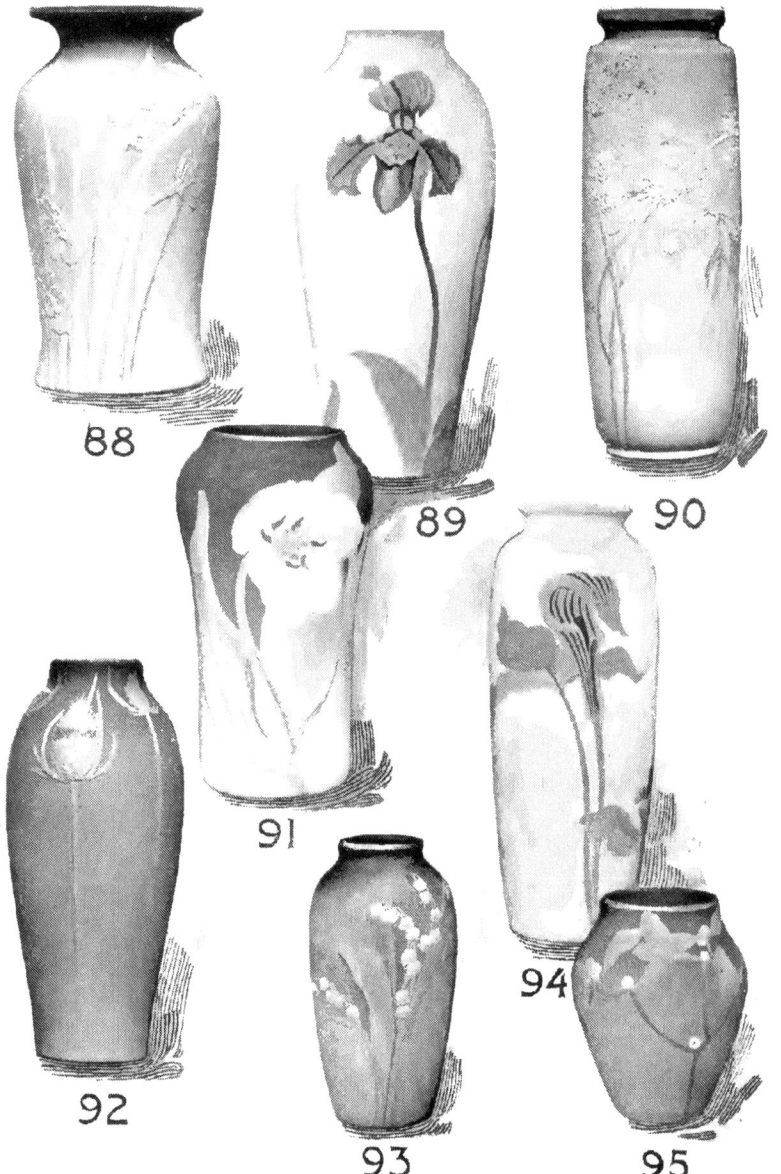

88

89

90

91

92

93

94

95

"VELLUM"

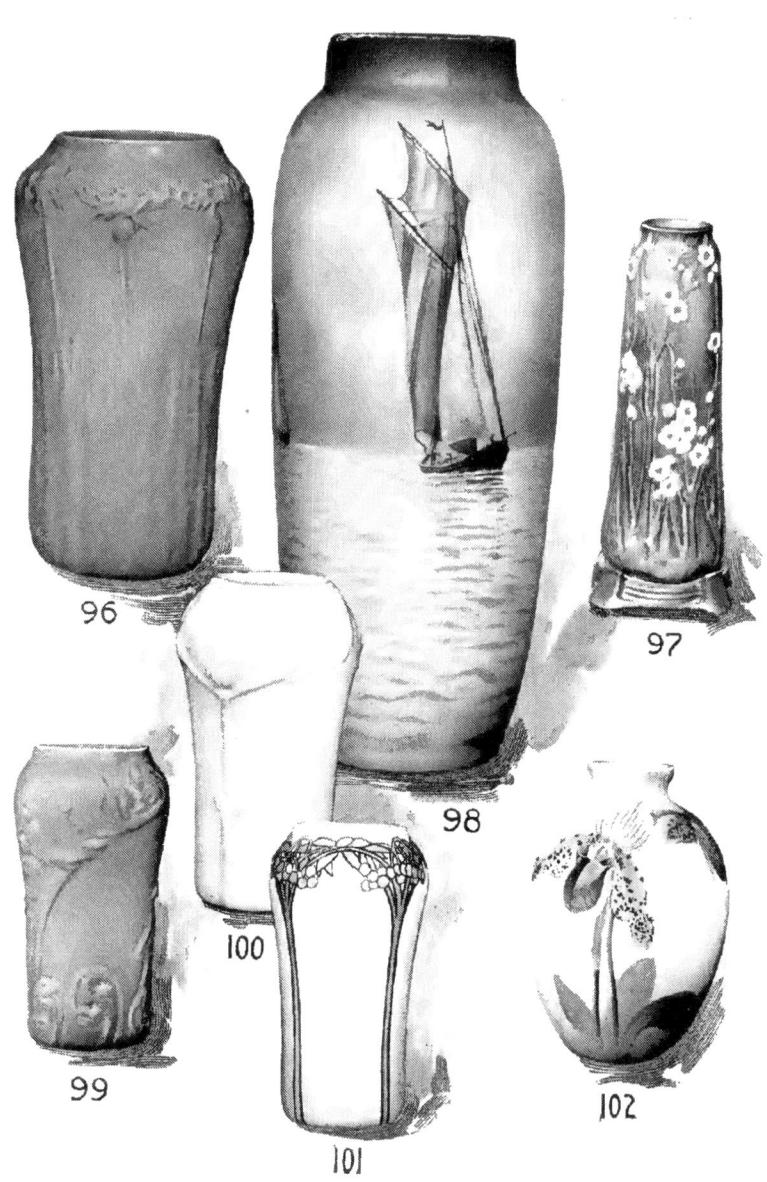

96

97

98

99

100

101

102

PRICE LIST

	IN. HIGH	PRICE
Sea Green Type Vase with fish decoration	9¾	$25.00
This shape is a simpler decoration		18 to 20
Standard Type Loving Cup with corn decoration	7¼	15.00
Modeled Mat Vase with Virginia Creeper in colored mat glazes	14	75.00
Iris Type Vase with poppy decoration	13½	100.00
Iris Type Vase with Iris decoration	6¾	10.00
Iris Type Vase with rose decoration	8¼	12 00
Iris Type Vase with lily of the valley design	6¾	8.00
Vellum Vase with white poppy design	8½	12.00
Mat Glaze Painting Vase with pink dogwood	5½	25.00
Incised Mat Vase	4¼	2.00
Incised Mat Vase	10½	7.00
Incised Mat Vase	4	2.00
Conventional Mat Glaze Vase with grape leaf design	5½	8.50
Conventional Mat Vase with rose design	5¾	4.00

NO.	TYPE	DESIGN	SIZE		PRICE
1	Standard	Milk Weed	8	in. high	$ 8.00
2	"	Grape	4¾ "	"	5.00
3	"	Pine Cones	11½ "	"	25.00
4	"	Teazel	10 "	"	10 to 12
5	"	Lily	6½ "	"	8.00
6	"	Blackberry Blossom	5¾ "	"	7.00
7	"	Cherry Blossoms	2¾ "	"	4.00
8	"	Clover Design	9 "	"	8 to 10
9	"		5¼ "	"	5.00
10	"		4¾ "	"	8.00
11	"	Sugar Bowl	3⅞ "	"	4.00
12	"	Creamer	2½ "	"	3.50
13	"	Night Blooming Cereus	13 "	"	20.00
14	"	Lily	14½ "	"	50.00
15	"	Japanese Flower	5½ "	"	3.50
16	"	Pansy	6¾ "	"	6.00
17	"	Pine Cones	10½ "	"	15.00
18	"	Oleander	8¾ "	"	10.00
19	"	Cherry Blossom	2½ "	"	3.00
20	"	Wild Carrot	6¼ "	"	5.00
21	Sea Green	Easter Lily	8 "	"	12.00
22	" "	Flower Decoraion	5¾ "	"	7.00
22	" "	Fish "	5¾ "	"	10.00
23	" "	Geese	10 "	"	50.00
24	" "	Water Lily	7 "	"	8 to 10

PRICE LIST

NO.	TYPE	DESIGN	SIZE	PRICE
25	Sea Green	Japanese Iris	10 in high	$30 00
26	Iris	White Poppies	10 " "	18 00
27	"	Iris	8 " "	12 00
28	"	Wistaria	8¾ " "	15.00
29	"	Bleeding Heart	9¾ " "	30 00
30	"	French Thistle	7 " "	8 to 10
31	"	Iris	7 " "	10.00
32	"	Orchid	14½ " "	100 to 150
33	"	Rose	9¾ " "	18 to 20
34	"	Orchid	10 " "	25 00
35	"	Iris	9¼ " "	20 00
36	"	Storks	16½ " "	150 to 200
37	"	Poppies	6½ " "	8 00
38	"	Jonquil	9½ " "	20 00
39	"	Clover	5¾ " "	6 to 7
40	"	Iris	6¾ " "	10 00
41	"	Mushrooms	9 " "	15 to 20
42	"	Mushrooms	4¾ " "	12 to 15
43	"	Grapes	6 " "	8 to 10
44	Mat Glaze Painting	Tulip	10 " "	35 00
45	" " "	Teazel	6¼ " "	12 to 15
46	" " "	Poppy	10 " "	30 00
47	" " "	Pink Dogwood	5½ " "	25 00
48	" " "	Lily	8 " "	20 00
49	Mat Glaze with Conventional Decoration in colors	Iris	9 " "	10 00
50	Mat Glaze with Conventional Decoration in colors	Poppy	11¼ " diam	15 00
51	Mat Glaze with Conventional Decoration in colors	Grape	7¼ " high	8 00
52	Mat Glaze with Conventional Decoration in colors	Dragon Fly	7¼ " diam	7 00
53	Mat Glaze with Conventional Decoration in colors	Cyclamen	5 " high	6 00
53	Mat Glaze with Conventional Decoration in colors		3½ " "	4 00
54	Incised Mat		7¾ " "	5 00
55	" "		6 " "	2 50
56	" "		5⅝ " "	2 50
57	"		6 " "	8 00
58	Modeled Mat	Jonquil	12	15 00
59	" "	Jonquil	8½ " "	15 00
60	" "	Clover Leaf	7 "	15 00
61	"	Dragon	13 " "	80 to 100
62	" "	Oak Leaves	10 " "	25 00
63	" "	Iris	8½ " "	40 00

PRICE LIST

NO.	TYPE	DESIGN	SIZE	PRICE
64	Incised Mat		5½ in. wide	$2.50
65	Modeled Mat		3 " "	1.00
66	" "	Grapes	15 " diam.	75 to 100
67	" "	Poppy	7½ " high	20.00
68	" "	Grapes	5⅝ " "	15.00
69	" "	Lobster	5⅝ " "	15 to 18
70	" "	Ivy	9 " "	20.00

LAMPS and ELECTROLIERS.

NO.	TYPE	DESIGN	SIZE	PRICE
71	Iris	Pine Cones	24 in. high	85.00
72	Modeled Mat Electrolier	Water Lily	14 " "	75.00
73	" " "	Thistle	22½ " "	85.00
74	Mat Glaze Candlestick		10½ " "	8.00
75	" " Lamp	{ Conventional Decoration in color }	33 " "	100.00
76	Modeled Mat Candlestick	Tulip	8¾ " "	25.00
77	Mat Glaze Lamp	{ Conventional Decoration in color }	22 " "	75.00
78	Modeled Mat Electrolier	Tulip	14 " "	75.00
79	Modeled and Painted Mat	{ with Special Modeled Base in metal }	24 " "	125.00
80	Vellum	Fish	9½ " "	25.00
81	"	Easter Lily	10½ " "	20.00
82	"	Conventional Fish	6½ " "	8 to 10
83	"	Jug	7½ " "	15.00
84	"	Modeled Lotus	7 " "	25.00
85	"	Orchid	6 " "	8 to 10
86	"	Conventional Dragon Fly	7½ " "	12.00
87	"	Dogwood	4¼ " "	8.00
88	"	Narcissus	8½ " "	15.00
89	"	Orchid	8¾ " "	15.00
90	"	Wild Carrot	7¾ " "	10 to 12
91	"	White Tulip	6½ " "	8 to 10
92	"	Teazel	7¼ " "	8 to 10
93	"	Lily of the Valley	5¾ " "	7 to 8
94	"	Jack-in-the-Pulpit	8 " "	12.00
95	"	Mistletoe	4¾ " "	7.00
96	"	Modeled Corn Flower	9 " "	18.00
97	"	{ Modeled Cherry Blossom with standard }	10 " "	25.00
98	"	Marine	10⅜ " "	25.00
98	"	with Flower Decoration		18.00
99	"	Modeled Fern Fronds	6½ " "	8 to 10
100	"	Modeled Mistletoe	7½ " "	12.00
101	"	Conventional Berry Design	6½ " "	10.00
102	"	Orchid	7½ " "	15 to 18

Milton Keynes UK
Ingram Content Group UK Ltd.
UKHW052217160823
426877UK00023B/239

9 781016 010368